Bébé

DAY BY DAY

Also by the Author

Bringing Up Bébé

Lust in Translation

Bébé
DAY BY DAY

100 Keys to French Parenting

Pamela Druckerman

THE PENGUIN PRESS
New York
2013

THE PENGUIN PRESS
Published by the Penguin Group
Penguin Group (USA) Inc., 375 Hudson Street,
New York, New York 10014, USA

USA · Canada · UK · Ireland · Australia
New Zealand · India · South Africa · China

Penguin Books Ltd, Registered Offices:
80 Strand, London WC2R 0RL, England
For more information about the Penguin Group visit penguin.com

First published in 2013 by The Penguin Press,
a member of Penguin Group (USA) Inc.

ISBN 978-1-59420-553-8

Printed in the United States of America
1   3   5   7   9   10   8   6   4   2

Designed by Nicole LaRoche
Illustrations © 2012 by Margaux Motin

For Simon and the individuals

Contents

Introduction

When I wrote a book about what I'd learned raising three kids in France, I wasn't sure that anyone besides my mother would read it. Actually, I wasn't even convinced that she would make it all the way through (she tends to prefer fiction).

But to my surprise, many nonrelatives read the book too. For a while there were lots of angry articles about it. Who was I to insult "American" parenting—if there really is such a thing? Surely there are lots of little French brats? Had I only researched rich Parisians? Was I extolling socialism—or worse—bottle feeding?

I'm the sort of person who hears any criticism of herself

and immediately thinks: that's so true! I fell into a funk. But then I started getting e-mails from regular American parents like me. (I've posted many of these e-mails on my Web site.) I quickly cheered up. They didn't think I'd falsely accused Americans of having a parenting problem. Like me, they were living that problem, and they were eager to hear about an alternative.

Some parents told me that the book validated what they had already been doing privately—and often guiltily. Others said they'd tried the book's methods on their kids, and that these really did work. (No one was more relieved to hear this than me.) Many asked for more tips and specifics, or for a version of the book—*sans* my personal backstory and voyage of discovery—that they could give as a kind of manual to grandparents, partners, and babysitters.

This is that book. The 100 "keys to French parenting" are my attempt to distill the smartest and most salient principles I've learned from French parents and experts. You don't have to live in Paris to apply them. You don't even have to like cheese. (Though you should have a look at the recipes at the end. They're a sample of what kids in French day cares eat, and they're delicious for grown-ups too.)

I believe in all 100 keys. But they're not my inventions or my personal proclamations. And they're not all right for everyone. The French are very clear that every child is different and that you should break the rules sometimes. As you read the keys, you'll start to notice that behind many of the individual tips are a few guiding principles. One of these principles was radical for me, as an American: If family life is centered entirely on children, it's not good for anyone, not even for the kids.

I think American parents have already figured this out. By now we've seen the statistics showing that as this new intensive style of parenting has taken hold—the one that's popped up seemingly out of nowhere in the last twenty years—marital satisfaction has fallen. Parents are famously less happy than nonparents, and they become even less happy with each additional child. (Working mothers in Texas apparently prefer housework to child care.) The most depressing study of middle-class American families I read described how parents have gone from being authority figures to being "valet[s] for the child." Given the amount of short-order cooking and shlepping that goes on, I would add "personal chefs" and "chauffeurs" too.

The clincher is that we're starting to doubt whether this demanding way of parenting is even good for kids. Many of our good intentions—from the baby brain-building videos to the all-consuming quest for college admittance—now seem to be of questionable value. Some experts call the first generation of kids to graduate from this brand of child rearing "teacups" because they're so fragile and warn that the way we're defining success is making these children unhappy.

Obviously, French parents don't do everything right. And they don't all do the same things. The keys describe the national conventional wisdom. It's what French parenting books, magazines, and experts widely say that you should do; and what most of the middle-class parents I know actually do, or at least believe they should be doing. (A French friend of mine said she planned to give a copy to her brother, so he could "become more French.")

A lot of "French" wisdom feels like common sense. I've

gotten letters from readers describing the overlaps between French parenting and Montessori, or the teachings of a Hungarian-born woman named Magda Gerber. Others assured me it's what we Americans did before Reaganomics, the psychotherapy boom, and that study saying that poor kids don't hear enough words when they're little. (Let's just say that the American upper-middle class massively overcompensated.)

Some French ideas have a power and elegance that's all their own. French parents to a great extent believe that babies are rational, that you should combine a little bit of strictness with a lot of freedom, and that you should listen carefully to children but not do everything they say. Their ability to move kids beyond "kid foods" is remarkable. Above all, the French think that the best parenting happens when you're calm. What's really neat is that, in France, you have an entire nation, in real time, trying to follow these principles. It's like a country-size control group. Come visit. You'll be amazed.

The main reason why French parenting is relevant to us now is that it's a kind of mirror image of what's been happening in America. We tend to think we should teach kids cognitive skills, such as reading, as soon as possible. They focus on "soft" skills like socializing and empathy in the early years. We want kids to be stimulated a lot; they think downtime is just as crucial. We often hesitate to frustrate a child; they think a child who can't cope with frustration will grow up miserable. We're focused on the outcomes of parenting; they think the quality of the eighteen years or so you spend living together counts for a lot too. We tend to think long-term interrupted sleep, routine tantrums, picky eating, and constant interruptions are mostly inevitable when you have little kids. They believe these things are—please imagine me saying this in a French accent—*impossible*.

I'm a journalist, not a parenting expert. So what really sold me on the French principles was the data. Many things that French parents do by intuition, tradition, or trial and error are exactly what the latest American research recommends. The French take for granted that you can teach little babies how to sleep through the night; that patience can be learned; that too much praise can be damaging for children; that you should become attuned to a baby's rhythms; that toddlers don't need flash cards; that tasting foods makes you like those foods—all things that science is telling us too. (To keep the keys simple, I've listed many of the relevant studies in the bibliography on page 141.)

Please take this book as inspiration, not doctrine. And be flexible. One of the French sayings I didn't have room for was "You have to keep changing what you do." Kids change quickly. When they do, you can keep the same guiding principles, but apply them differently. I hope that this book helps make that possible. Rather than giving lots of specific rules, it's more like a toolbox to help parents figure things out on their own. As the old saying goes: Don't give a man a *filet de saumon à la vapeur de fenouil.* Just teach him how to fish.

And don't worry about socialism. American parenting is changing, as it always does. But whatever our next phase is, it won't be French (or Chinese or Icelandic). It'll be our own home brew. I'm delighted to toss in some ideas. My mother, at least, thinks I'm on to something.

Chapter One

A Croissant
in the Oven

All pregnant women worry. You're making a human being, after all. Some of us can barely make dinner. But in America, worrying can become an Olympic sport. We feel we must weigh whether each bite of food we eat is in the baby's best interest. All this angst doesn't feel pleasant. But often, it does feel necessary. We're signaling that there's nothing we won't sacrifice for our unborn child.

The French don't valorize a pregnant woman's anxiety. Instead, in the word cloud of French pregnancy, terms like *serenity, balance,* and *Zen* keep popping up. Mothers-to-be are supposed to signal their competence by showing how calm they are and by making it clear that they still experience pleasure. This small shift in emphasis makes a very big difference.

1. *Pregnancy Is Not an Independent Research Project*

French mothers-to-be might read a baby book or two. But they don't consider this required reading or feel that they must pick a parenting philosophy. There is an important difference between being prepared and being the person who recites the names of chromosomal disorders at dinner.

Making a baby is more mysterious and meaningful than anything you've ever done (unless you've previously been pregnant, or had cats). You can dwell in the enormity of that without trying to micromanage it, and without anointing a personal guru. The most important voice to have inside your head is your own.

2. Calm Is Better for the Baby

If you're not persuaded to be calm for your own sake, do it for your unborn child. French pregnancy magazines say that the fetus senses his mother's moods. He's jolted by too much stress, and soothed when pleasure hormones cross the placenta. Experts urge pregnant women to reduce worry by discussing their concerns with a doctor or therapist and by pampering themselves with pedicures, romantic nights out (preferably with the baby's father), and lunch with friends. In the French telling, the resulting *zen maman* pops out a *zen bébé*, and a calm pregnancy sets the tone for calm parenting.

3. Don't Panic About Sushi

France's future *mamans* try to keep the risks in perspective. They know that some things—like cigarettes and alcohol—are categorically hazardous to the unborn child. French doctors now advise going cold turkey on both (though some women still have the occasional *coupe de champagne*). But other things are dangerous only if they happen to be contaminated. Sushi, salami, uncooked shellfish, and unpasteurized cheese are in this category.

Please don't rush out and eat oysters. Listen to your doctor. But remember that accidentally eating unpasteurized Parmesan cheese with your pasta is not grounds for a nervous breakdown.

4. The Fetus Doesn't Need Cheesecake

Don't view pregnancy as the culinary free-for-all you've been saving up for through all those food-deprived years of courtship and marriage. French guides say that when your body shouts for brioche, you should distract it by eating an apple or a piece of cheese. Women's long-term strategy is to enjoy the occasional bowl of *mousse au chocolat*, instead of banishing it entirely. This quells the beast, and makes them less likely to go overboard on such foods later. This way of eating—moderation instead of deprivation—could explain why a recent French pregnancy book was called *Emergency: She Wants Strawberries.*

5. Eat for One (and a Bit)

Plan to emerge from pregnancy with your allure intact. Take your doctor's weight-gain limits seriously. (The French limits are lower than American ones, and French-women treat them like holy edicts.) Remember that it will be much easier to lose the baby weight if you haven't gained too much while pregnant. One French guide says that a moderately active pregnant woman needs an additional two hundred to five hundred calories per day, but warns that anything more "inevitably turns into fat." This needn't feel austere. Crucially, Frenchwomen don't eat merely to nourish the fetus. They also believe that they're entitled to enjoy themselves.

6. Don't Borrow Your Husband's Shirts

Dressing like a shapeless blob is bad for morale (yours and your mate's; possibly even the baby's). Invest strategically in a few flattering maternity clothes. Then convert cardigans and leggings from your closet into pregnancy gear and brighten your face with lipstick and colored scarves. Attention to these details signals that you are not graduating from "*femme*" to "*maman.*" You'll be both.

7. Stay Sexual

French pregnancy magazines don't just mention that it's okay to have sex. They spell out exactly how to do it—including lists of pregnancy-safe sex toys (nothing with batteries), aphrodisiacs (mustard, cinnamon, and chocolate), and detailed instructions on how to maneuver yourself into third-trimester positions. Accompanying fashion spreads show pregnant women in lacy maternity lingerie with come-hither looks. Some of this is aspirational. Pregnant Frenchwomen don't morph into sex goddesses; they have the same fluctuating libidos as the rest of us. But they don't assume that they've crossed into a realm where even the appearance of intimacy is optional. They know that if you put your seductive powers in the deep freeze, it's hard to thaw them out later.

8. Epidurals Aren't Evil

The French don't view childbirth as a heroic journey in pain tolerance, or early proof of the trials a mother is willing to undergo for her child. Frenchwomen don't typically launch their babies into the world amid a frenzy of micromanagement in which they specify the lighting, the guest list, and who gets to "catch" the baby when it comes out.

There are midwives, prenatal baby whisperers, and even some home births in France. The French don't think there's anything wrong with giving birth the way you want to. But they maintain that the point is to get the baby safely from your uterus into your arms. While some things may be better *au naturel* (breasts and maple syrup come to mind), others are better with a giant dose of drugs. Even Frenchwomen who subsist on organic food and plan to breast-feed well into preschool are delighted when the anesthesiologist arrives.

9. Don't Stand on the Business End

Dads: Unless you are actually delivering the baby, don't stand at the "end of the tunnel." Yes, there's the miracle of life to witness. Of course you want to seem welcoming to your child. But consider meeting him half a second later, in order to preserve your partner's feminine mystique. It gets messy down there. As the French saying goes, Not all truths should be told.

Chapter Two

Bébé Einstein

The French believe that babies aren't helpless blobs. They treat even newborns like tiny, rational people who understand language and can learn things (when they're taught gently and at their own pace). This isn't as far-fetched as it sounds. American scientists have recently proven that babies aren't blank slates; they can make moral judgments and do basic math. Who knows what baby superpowers they'll discover next? At the very least, we should remember that when we talk, they might be listening.

10. Give Your Baby a House Tour

Like anyone entering her new home for the first time, your baby wants to get oriented, and know where she'll be sleeping. When you bring her back from the hospital, show her around. This is it: home base! Later, make a practice of saying good-bye to her when you're going out and telling her when you'll be back. Help her make sense of the world by explaining that grandma is daddy's (or mommy's) mother, and what that new sound is outside. The French believe that when they speak to a baby, they're not just reassuring her with the sound of a parent's voice; they're conveying important information. They think that explaining things to an upset baby can calm her down.

11. Observe Your Baby

When you ask a new French mom to explain her parenting philosophy, she'll often shrug and say: "I just observe my baby." She means that she literally spends a lot of time

watching what the baby does. This is more important—
and less obvious—than it sounds. She's trying to tune in to
the baby's experience, and learn to read and follow her
cues. (American scientists call this sensitivity, and say it's
one of the most important qualities in a caregiver.) The
idea is that you want to be there when the baby needs you.
But when she's happily singing and drooling on the play
mat, try to just let her be. You are striving to achieve what
the French call *complicité*—mutual trust and understanding, even with someone who regularly throws up on you.

12. Tell Your Baby the Truth

France's most famous parenting expert, Françoise Dolto,
said that children don't need family life to be perfect. But
they do need it to be coherent, and not secret. She insisted
that babies can sense when there's a problem in the home
and need the same comforting confirmation we all do:
"You're not nuts! Something really is wrong!" Dolto said
that from six months old, parents should tell the baby if

they're getting divorced. When a grandparent dies, parents should gently explain this, and briefly bring the child to the funeral. An adoptee needs to hear about her birth mother, even if her adoptive mother simply says: "I don't know her, but you knew her." The French believe that from the time a child is small, parents can make situations easier to accept just by making them clear.

13. Be Polite

French parents tend not to speak down to their infants in singsongy baby talk. However they do pay them the courtesy of saying "*bonjour*," "please," and "thank you." If the baby understands you, it's never too early to start modeling good manners. And this early *politesse* sets the tone for calm and respectful relations later.

14. Don't Stimulate Her All the Time

Of course you should talk to your baby, show her things, and read her books. But a baby, like anyone else, needs downtime. She doesn't want to be constantly watched and spoken to. She needs time to assimilate all the new information she's been taking in. (Her parents need it too.) Let interactions and conversations follow a natural rhythm. Give the baby time to roll around in a safe space and be free.

15. Nudge Him onto a Schedule

For the first few months, French parents usually feed babies on demand. After that, they take a few things for granted:

- The baby should eat at more or less the same times each day.
- A few big feeds are better than lots of small ones.

- The baby should adjust to the family's regular eating rhythm.

With these ideas in mind, you can gradually stretch out the amount of time between feedings. Distract the baby from pangs of hunger by taking her for a walk or strapping her into a carrier. At the beginning, you might gain only a few minutes a day. But she'll get used to waiting a bit. Eventually she'll get to three hours between feeds, and before long to four. Soon she'll be on more or less the same eating rhythm she'll be on for the rest of her life: breakfast, lunch, and dinner, plus an afternoon snack. (This roughly corresponds to 8:00 a.m., noon, 4:00 p.m., and 8:00 p.m., but the schedule isn't observed with military precision.)

16. Baby Formula Isn't Poison

French mothers know that breast is best. But they don't view breast-feeding as a measure of the mom, or keep nursing through Danteesque trials of pain and inconvenience.

Many pragmatically point out that they themselves are healthy, despite having drunk a lot of powdered formula— the old, worse formula (there are other factors, but still). Some guilt is encroaching in France. But Frenchwomen still tend to think it's unhealthy and unpleasant to breast-feed under moral duress. They believe that whether and how long to nurse should be your private decision, not your play group's. The best reason to breast-feed, they say, is if you and your baby enjoy it.

17. Make Vegetables a Child's First Food

If your baby's first food is bland rice cereal, she'll probably take to it. But why not start with something more exciting? From about six months, French parents feed babies flavor-packed pureed spinach, carrots, seeded zucchini, and other vegetables. They soon move on to fruits, small amounts of meat, and different types of fish. They're trying to launch their children on a lifelong relationship with these flavors, and introduce them to the pleasures of eating.

Chapter Three

Rock-a-Bye Bébé

ere's a French paradox: French babies often sleep through the night by three or four months old, or even sooner. Yet their parents don't make them "cry it out" for hours on end.

This isn't a coincidence, a mystery, or the result of adding Cognac to their milk. If you believe that little babies can learn things, then you can teach them things. And one of the things you can teach them, early on, is how to sleep.

18. Understand the Science of Sleep

Your baby is unique and adorable and will one day be accepted to a high school of performing arts. There will undoubtedly be a biopic about his life, in which an aging Gwyneth Paltrow plays you, his elderly but still ravishing mother. However, as French parents know, even your own baby is subject to the laws of science. And one of these laws is that all healthy babies, even yours, sleep in brief cycles. At the end of each cycle, babies often wake up and cry a bit.

The key to sleeping for longer stretches is for the baby to learn how to connect his sleep cycles on his own. He needs to be able to wake up after one cycle then plunge into the next one without anyone else having to get out of bed. Grown-ups—except for the insomniacs and menopausal among us—manage this same feat every night.

Connecting sleep cycles is a skill. A few lucky babies are born with it. Most have to practice before they master it.

19. Babies Are Noisy Sleepers

Infants make a lot of noise when they sleep. They whine. They move their arms like traffic cops. This does not mean they are awake. If you instantly race in to their rooms or pick them up each time they make a peep, you will sometimes wake them up.

20. Do "The Pause"

We know that babies often cry when they're learning to connect their sleep cycles. We also know that they can make a noise like an angry frog and yet still be asleep. So from the time the baby is a few weeks old, pause a bit when he cries at night.*

You are waiting to see if, this time, your baby will have a breakthrough moment and plunge into the next sleep

---

*When you get to know your baby's cries better, you might come to recognize his get-me-out-of-this-wet-diaper cry. When you hear that one, you don't need to pause—just change him.

cycle on his own, without anyone else's help. If you immediately rush in and pick him up, he won't have a chance to develop this skill.

Maybe the baby isn't ready to connect his cycles yet. But if you don't pause, you won't know, and neither will the baby. He'll think he needs you to put him back to sleep at the end of each cycle. Rushing in may make you feel like a devoted and sacrificial parent. But in effect you're treating your baby like a helpless blob who is not ready to learn and grow. Also, the baby might just be making noises in his sleep. So if you go in and pick him up, you might—despite your excellent intentions—actually wake him up.

You needn't pause for very long. Some French parents wait five minutes or so. Others wait a bit more, or less. They're not letting the baby cry it out. If after these few minutes he's still crying, they reason that he must need something. Then they pick him up.

21. Get Baby in the Mood to Sleep

The Pause is necessary but not sufficient to teach babies how to sleep. The French believe you should also have rituals that set the tone for bedtime. Keep the baby near daylight during the day, even when he's napping. Signal to him that the big nighttime sleep is approaching by giving him a bath, changing him into pajamas, singing him a lullaby, and actually saying "good night." Once he's calm and relaxed but preferably still awake, put him to bed in a dark room at night. Spending cozy time together before bed matters. You want to send him off to sleep feeling secure enough that he can separate from you for a little while, and still be okay.

22. Try the Talking Cure

Why talk to everyone else about how your baby sleeps except the baby himself? Tell him it's bedtime. Explain that the whole family needs rest. Say that you're going to pause a few minutes before you come in to him, because you want him to be able to fall back asleep on his own. Tell him how nice it will be for everyone—including him—when he no longer needs to wake up at 3:00 a.m. One French baby book says that after a baby sleeps through the night for the first time, his parents should tell him how pleased and proud they are. Doing this also helps lock in the baby's newfound ability.

23. Sleeping Well Is Better for the Baby

French parents don't sleep-teach babies just for their own convenience. They also believe that sleeping well is in a child's best interest. Research backs them up: a child who sleeps poorly can become hyperactive and irritable, have trouble learning and remembering things, and have more accidents. (My personal studies suggest that the same is true for sleep-deprived mothers.)

And sleep contains an important symbolic lesson for babies: learning to sleep is part of learning to be part of the family. Babies eventually need to adapt to what others need too. Three months—the age when many French babies sleep through the night—happens to be about when French maternity leave ends and many *mamans* need to be fresh for work in the morning.

24. Don't Expect Any of This to Work Immediately

It probably won't. But stick with it and stay confident that your baby will, as the French say, "do his nights." Convey this confidence to your baby (it helps!). Believe that if you keep gently and patiently teaching your baby how to sleep well, he will eventually learn—often just when your own sleep-deprivation experiment starts to feel unbearable.

25. If You Miss the Window for the Pause, Let Baby Cry It Out

....

The gentle sleep-teaching method of The Pause works best in the baby's first four months. When parents miss this window, French experts often suggest doing some form of crying it out—leaving the baby to cry for a longer period. Talk to the baby about this too. It generally succeeds within a few nights.

Chapter Four

Bébé Gourmet

magine a planet where family mealtimes are pleasant, children eat the same foods as their parents, and few kids get fat. That planet is France. But none of this happens automatically. French parents set out to teach their kids how to eat well, and they work at it assiduously. Their efforts pay off four times a day. The moral of the French food story is: treat your child like a little gourmet, and he will (gradually) rise to the occasion.

26. There Are No "Kid" Foods

You can find chicken nuggets, fish fingers, and pizza in France. But these are occasional foods for kids, typically not daily fare (the same goes for French fries—known locally as *frites*). Parents almost never let their kids become picky eaters who survive on mono-diets of pasta and white rice. Starting from a very young age, French kids mostly eat the same foods as their parents. The weekly menu at Paris's state-run day care consists of four-course meals (including a cheese course) that look like something you might order in a bistro (see the sample weekly crèche menu on page 135).

27. There's One Snack a Day

I used to find it hard to imagine kids going from breakfast to lunch without as much as a raisin in between. But it turns out this feat is possible, and can even be pleasant.

French kids typically eat only at mealtimes and at the afternoon snack, called the *goûter* (pronounced "goo-tay").

It turns out that if the kid doesn't snack much, she's actually hungry by mealtimes, so she eats more. There's also something calming about not regarding every moment as a potential eating opportunity. Everyone can get on with other things. And once you're in the swing of this one-snack system, the *goûter* becomes a special little occasion every day. It's usually some combination of sweets, dairy, and fruit. Often there's some chocolate. One classic *goûter* is a chocolate sandwich—a piece of dark chocolate in a baguette. It might come with a box of juice.

28. Don't Solve a Crisis with a Cookie

Not producing an Oreo whenever a child whines can have far-reaching benefits. First, you're not rewarding her outbursts, so you're not encouraging her to whine again. Second, you're teaching her not to eat just because she's upset.

She'll thank you when she's thirty and can still fit into her high school jeans.

29. You Are the Keeper of the Fridge

In France, kids don't have the right to open the refrigerator and take whatever they want. They have to ask their parents first. This doesn't just cut down on the snacking in the house. It also cuts down on the chaos.

30. Let Kids Cook

The five-year-old French girl who lives next door to us measures and mixes the oil, vinegar, mustard, and salt for the family's vinaigrette all by herself. It's no coincidence that she loves salad. We all feel more invested in foods that we've had a hand in preparing. (Just think how much you want everyone to taste your casserole at Thanksgiving.)

I've seen French two-year-olds sit at the kitchen counter tearing up spinach. Three-year-olds learn to peel cucumbers, cut tomatoes with a blunt-tipped knife, and mix the batter for crepes. Parents oversee this process, and don't mind a little mess. Plus there's no better time to find out what happened to your kindergartner at school than when you are peeling the shells off hard-boiled eggs together.

When the cooking is done, eat as the French typically do: together, at the table, with the television off.

31. Serve Food in Courses, Vegetables First

Family meals don't need to be fancy. You don't need to light candles or drape a white napkin over your arm. Just bring out some vegetables first, before anything else. If your kids haven't been snacking all day, they will be hungry and more likely to eat them. (The same strategy works at breakfast with cut-up fruit.) A vegetable starter doesn't have to be elaborate. It can be a bowl of peas in pods (all the better to shell them), some cut-up cherry tomatoes with salt and olive oil, or sautéed broccoli. Just put a serving on each child's plate, and wait.

32. Everyone Eats the Same Thing

In France, children don't decide what they'll have for dinner. There are no choices or customizations. There's just one meal, the same one for everyone. It's safe to try this at home. If a child doesn't eat something, or barely eats it, react neutrally. Do not offer her something else instead. If she is just emerging from a kids' food ghetto, ease her into it by making family meals that everyone likes, then gradually introducing new dishes.

Above all, stay positive and calm. Give the new rules time to settle. Remember that you're crediting your child with being able to eat the same foods as you. Accompany the new rules with some new freedoms, like letting her cut the quiche, or sprinkle the Parmesan cheese herself. When you eat in a restaurant, let her order what she wants, within reason.

33. *You Just Have to Taste It*

Most kids like ice cream instantly (though mine strangely complained that it was "too cold"). However, many other foods take some warming up to. Their very newness puts kids off. It's only through trying these foods lots of times that kids start to like them.

This is the cornerstone of the way the French feed their children. Kids have to take at least one bite of every dish that's on the table. I'm sure there are French families who don't consider this rule to be sacred and infallible, but I have yet to meet them.

Present the tasting rule to your child as if it's a law of nature—like gravity. Explain that our tastes are shaped by what we eat. If she's nervous about tasting something for the first time, let her just pick up a piece and sniff it (often a little nibble will follow). One new food per meal is enough. Serve it alongside something you know she likes.

Oversee this process without acting like a prison guard. Be calm and even playful about it. After she takes the requisite bite, acknowledge this. React neutrally if she says she doesn't like it. Never offer a replacement food. Remember, you're playing the long game. You don't want her to eat an artichoke once, under duress. You want her to gradually learn to like artichokes.

34. Keep Foods in the Rotation

Even if a certain food isn't a hit, make sure it keeps coming back. Put broccoli in soup, melt some cheese on it, or stir-fry it. Broccoli might never be your daughter's favorite food. But with each taste, it will get closer to being part of her repertoire. She'll come to regard it as normal. Once it's solidly established, keep it in the mix. Ultimately, your child won't love all foods. But she'll give each one a chance.

35. You Choose the Foods,
She Chooses the Quantities

A child knows (or should learn to know) when she's had enough. Serve smallish portions, and don't pressure her to finish. Wait and see if she asks for seconds before serving more. If she asks for a third helping of pasta, offer her a yogurt or some cheese instead. Sweeten the deal by letting her add some honey or a spoonful of jam to plain yogurt. After that, let her choose a fresh fruit or a fruit puree (like those small containers of unsweetened applesauce).

The goal isn't to cajole enough nutrients into a child's mouth at every sitting. It's to guide her into becoming an independent eater who enjoys food and regulates her own appetite. If she doesn't eat enough at one meal, she'll catch up at the next one. If she's always snacking, she'll never learn to eat at mealtimes.

36. Variety, Variety

The French are nuts about variety. They serve kids lots of different foods, prepared lots of different ways. They aim for a variety of textures and colors too. This has many benefits:

- Kids get a variety of nutrients. They're more likely to eat a balanced diet if they eat lots of different foods.
- It makes mealtimes more peaceful. If your kids are used to different foods, you don't have to be terrified that a picky eater will erupt at the sight of an herb in her soup.
- It's more social. You can take your kid anywhere and she'll find something she likes. You won't have to keep apologizing to hosts who don't serve plain pasta. You build complicity with your child as you roll with it together.
- It's more pleasurable for the child. Her world expands as she discovers different tastes, smells, and textures.

- It shows your confidence in your child. If you treat her like a budding food adventurer, she'll eventually live up to your expectations. Whereas if you treat her like a finicky eater who can handle only grilled cheese and the occasional banana, that's what she'll become.

37. Drink Water

In France, chilled or lukewarm water is the de facto drink at lunch and dinner (and anytime in between). Parents typically don't take drink orders; they just put a pitcher of water on the table. (This quickly becomes a habit.) Juice is for breakfast, and for the occasional afternoon snack. Sugary drinks are for special occasions like parties. Period. *Santé!*

38. Looks Matter

Everyone is more drawn to food that looks appetizing. In Parisian restaurants, almost as much thought goes into presenting food as into cooking it. That can be your principle at home too. Put takeout on serving plates. Garnish a monotone dinner with cherry tomatoes or some grated carrots. Enlist kids to arrange raw vegetables on a platter, or assemble colorful sandwich melts, which you then broil in the oven. From two or three years old, all kids can eat on ceramic plates and drink out of small glasses, as French kids do.

39. Talk About Food

French people talk a lot about food. That's part of how they convey to kids that eating isn't just for nutrition—it's a full-on sensory experience. Food guides suggest getting beyond "I like it" / "I don't like it" and instead asking questions such as: Are the apples sour or sweet? How does

mackerel taste different from salmon? Which is better—
red-leaf lettuce or arugula?

Treat food as an endless conversation starter. When the
cake collapses or the stew is a disaster, laugh about it
together.

At the supermarket, take a walking tour of the produce
department, and let your kid choose some fruits and vegetables (one of my sons likes to ride in the shopping cart
wielding a giant leek).

Above all, keep the food chat positive. If your child
abruptly announces that she doesn't like pears anymore,
calmly ask what she's decided to like instead.

40. Have the Day's Nutritional Balance in Mind

French parents carry around a little mental map of what
their kids eat each day. They expect them to get most of
their protein at lunchtime, whereas dinner will center on
grains and vegetables. Kids typically eat sugary foods for

dessert with lunch or at the *goûter*. Dinnertime dessert is usually yogurt, cheese, or fruit. ("What you eat in the evening just stays with you for years," one French mother explained to me.)

41. Dinner Shouldn't Involve Hand-to-Hand Combat

A French nutritionist says her best advice is this: Don't let your child see how desperately you want him to eat his vegetables.

Don't puff up with exaggerated food cheer either. Play it cool. Those haricots verts you've just placed on the table are not the second coming. The tone you're aiming for at mealtimes is cheerful nonchalance. Just be calmly positive about food. Tell kids that meals are a time for the whole family to be together and enjoy one another's company.

42. Eat Chocolate

Don't treat candy like it's kryptonite, or try to pretend that refined sugar doesn't exist. That will just make kids more likely to go overboard when they finally get their hands on some. Instead, teach them that sweets are occasional pleasures to enjoy in controlled doses. French kids eat small helpings of chocolate or cookies on a regular basis, usually at the afternoon *goûter*. They often eat cake on weekends, just not too much. On birthdays and at school parties, parents tend to give kids free rein. We all need some time away from the regular rules.

43. Keep Meals Short and Sweet

Dinner is not a hostage situation. Don't expect young kids to stay at the table for longer than twenty or thirty minutes. When they ask to be liberated, let them go. With age comes longer meals.

In restaurants, leaving the table usually isn't an option.

Plan these outings carefully. Make sure that children arrive hungry and not exhausted. Bring some books or drawing supplies. Before you go inside, explain even to little children that special rules apply—one of which is that they can choose what they'll eat. Remind them to be *sage*—calm and in control of themselves. (Unlike the English equivalent, "Be good," this implies a certain wisdom and capacity for self-control.)

Chapter Five

Sooner Isn't Better

t is tempting to think of early childhood as the start of a marathon in which the finish line is admission to a university (winners get to go to the Ivy League). In this analogy, you'd want your kids off to a fast start—to begin talking, reading, and doing math as soon as possible. You'd give them flashcards, brain-building toys, and maybe a special contraption to help them learn to walk.

The French want their kids to be successful too. (They have their own version of the Ivy League, called the *grandes écoles*.) But they probably wouldn't use the marathon analogy. They don't tend to think there's any point in rushing little kids through developmental milestones, or teaching them skills like reading and math before they are most ready for them. French preschoolers learn some letters, but they don't actually learn to read until the equivalent of first grade—about age six. (Teenagers in Finland have the highest average reading and math scores in the Western world, and kids there don't learn to read until they're seven.)

The latest American research validates this slower approach. It turns out that it's more important to teach preschoolers skills like concentration, getting along with others, and self-control (more about self-control in chapter 6). These abilities—more than math worksheets or preliteracy training—create a strong basis for later academic success. And as the French can affirm, avoiding the baby marathon is a lot more pleasant for both parents and kids.

44. Don't Teach Your Toddler How to Read

Yes, it's technically possible to teach three-year-olds how to recognize words. But what's the rush? You don't want to take time away from teaching children the things they most need to learn at that age, like how to be organized, articulate, and empathetic. French preschools teach kids how to have conversations, finish projects, and tackle problems. In my daughter's Parisian kindergarten class one day, the assignment was for twenty-five illiterate five-year-olds to give talks on "justice" or "courage." When these kids are six, they'll learn to read in much less time than it would take to teach them at three.

45. Don't Rush the Developmental Stages

The French have a saying: "You can't go faster than the music." They believe that a child will roll over, rise up, get potty-trained, and start to talk when he's good and ready. Parents should lovingly encourage and support him—not turn his childhood into boot camp. Anyway, being a little kid shouldn't be hard work. There's time enough for that later.

46. Teach the Four Magic Words

We Americans have "please" and "thank you." The French have those plus two more: "hello" and "good-bye." They're especially zealous about making a child say *"bonjour"* as soon as he walks into someone's house. He doesn't get to slouch in under the cover of his parents' greeting.

French parents view *bonjour* as a critical lesson in empathy. Saying it forces a child out of his selfish bubble, and makes him realize that other people have needs and feelings too—such as the simple need to be acknowledged. *Bonjour* also sets the tone for him to observe other rules of civility. If he says *"bonjour,"* he's less likely to jump on the couch. He's been counted as a person; a little person, but a person nonetheless.

47. Let Kids "Awaken" and "Discover"

Centuries of great French art, cooking, and design have left their mark on French parenting. Today's French parents teach kids about sensory pleasures like tasting new foods, "discovering" their bodies through movement (Americans might call this exercise), or "awakening" to new sensations like splashing in a pool (this comes long before French children actually learn to swim). Awakening often doesn't require much hard work from parents. It can come from rolling around on a picnic blanket and studying the grass. Awakening probably helps forge some neural pathways. But the real point is to teach children how to enjoy just being in the world.

48. Encourage Insouciance

A few music classes are fine. But try to give little kids lots of free time just to play. "When the child plays, he constructs himself," one of my daughter's Parisian day-care teachers explained. (By design, the day care gives kids large quantities of unstructured time.) The latest science seems to side with the French. A roundup of neuroscience research couldn't say enough about the benefits of exploratory play: it teaches kids persistence, relationship skills, and creative problem solving; it improves their attention spans and their confidence; and it gives them a chance to master activities. But playing isn't just developmentally important; it's also fun.

49. Let Your Child Socialize with Other Kids

You know how you crave adult company after being alone with a three-year-old all day? Well, just imagine how that three-year-old feels—in reverse. French mothers want to spend time with their offspring. But they also think it's crucial that kids socialize with people who are equally enchanted by fire engines and princess paraphernalia. They want their children to learn how to make friends, to wait their turns, and to get along in a group. Middle- and upper-middle-class working parents would rather put their children in high-quality day care than leave them at home alone with a nanny.

50. Back Off at the Playground

French parents believe that once a child can walk on his own and safely climb up the slide, their job is to watch from the sidelines as he plays. At French playgrounds, you don't see parents narrating a child's every move, going down the slide behind their kids, or automatically leaping to their child's defense in every dispute. They give him a chance to work out conflicts on his own.

Resist the urge to cross wobbly wooden bridges or to provide constant commentary and encouragement. Just sit on a bench, watch, and recharge. That way you'll be a lot more joyful and patient when he does need you.

51. Do Extracurriculars for Pleasure

You're not building a bionic child. Do not give him violin lessons or read him the twelfth book of the day merely to help him gain hypothetical IQ points. Choose activities that your child enjoys, then do them at a natural pace. Read the child-development studies if you want, but don't let them plan your child's day.

52. It's Not Just About Outcomes

Yes, it's a competitive world. Of course you want to position your offspring to beat out that trilingual rug rat next door. But childhood is not merely preparation for the future. The quality of the nearly two decades you're spending together matters too. Learn to identify and enjoy what the French call *moments privilégiés*, little pockets of joy or calm when you simply appreciate being together.

Chapter Six

Wait a Minute

One reason why French family life often feels calm is that parents emphasize patience. They don't treat waiting—and related skills, like coping with frustration and delaying gratification—as innate qualities that kids are born with (or without). They believe these can be learned. French parents aim to teach their kids patience, the same way they will later teach them how to ride a bicycle.

Also, they find the alternative intolerable. French parents can imagine a world in which they could never finish a phone call or a cup of coffee, and where kids collapse each time they're denied a candy bar. They've seen children who regularly go from calm to hysterical in seconds, and make everyone miserable in their wakes. They don't want to live in that world or think it's inevitable to do so. And they don't think that living there would make children happy either.

53. Give Kids Lots of Chances to Practice Waiting

The secret to patience isn't expecting a child to be a stoic who freezes and silently waits. Scientists have found that kids become good at waiting once they learn how to distract themselves—by inventing a little song or burping at themselves in the mirror, for instance. This makes the waiting bearable.

French parents have discovered this too. They know that they don't even have to teach a child how to distract himself. If they simply say "wait" a lot (*attend* in French) and make a child practice waiting on a daily basis, she'll figure out how to distract herself. But if they drop everything the instant she complains that she's bored, or if they get off the phone when she interrupts, the child isn't going to get good at waiting. She's going to get good at whining.

54. Slow Down Your Response Times

Embrace a French pace of life. When you're busy scrambling eggs and your daughter asks you to inspect her tower of toilet paper rolls, explain nicely that you'll be there in a few minutes. At dinner, don't leap up to grab a napkin the moment she demands it (or, better yet, put the napkins on a low shelf so she can get one herself). When you're busy, politely point out to your child what you're doing, and ask her to take it in.

This doesn't just make life calmer. It's also what the French call an obligatory passage for the child, when she learns that she's not the center of the universe. Parents believe that a child who doesn't realize this—and who feels she's entitled to anything she wants—won't see any reason to grow up.

The French have reasonable expectations. They wouldn't

ask a young child to sit through Shakespeare (or Molière). They just want her to be able to wait a few seconds, or a few minutes. Slowing things down even this little bit will make her better at coping with boredom, and take the panicky edge off things. Patience is a muscle. The more a child plays on her own, the better she gets at it.

55. Treat Kids as if They Can Control Themselves

Play to the top of a child's intelligence. Expect her not to grab things, and to be able to put all her Legos back in their box. Get down on the floor and gently tell a toddler who's pulling books off the shelf that she should stop, and show her how to put them back. When she tosses grapes on the floor, show her how to keep them on her plate. Do this patiently and face-to-face. A child needs to learn the limits, but she also needs love. "It takes both love and frustration for the child to construct himself," one expert explains. If you give the child just love without limits, she'll soon become a little tyrant (the French call this an *enfant roi*—a child king).

56. Don't Let Your Child Interrupt You

When a child interrupts (assuming she's not hemorrhaging), French parents believe that you should calmly say some version of "I'm in the middle of speaking to someone. Please wait and I'll be with you in a moment." Then make good on that promise. Continue your conversation, but when you've finished, turn back to the child and listen to her. Have her wait her turn to speak at the dinner table too, and teach her at least to say "excuse me" if it's urgent. (*Urgent* in our house usually means that the dragon's second head—the less important head, I keep saying—has fallen off again.)

Remember that you're not just trying to enjoy the simple pleasure of completing a thought. You're also teaching your child to respect others and to be aware of what's happening around her. One Frenchwoman says that when her son interrupts, she has him look at the person she's speaking to so that he fully registers what's going on. "It's a way of living together," she explains. All this practice won't prevent your child from ever interrupting again. But she'll gradually get more in touch with the rhythm of the room.

57. Don't Interrupt Your Child

Everyone in the house has a right to be absorbed in something without being interrupted. When a child is happily caught up in an activity, parents should try not to come charging over with a question or a change of plans. When people aren't bursting in on one another, the whole pace of family life slows down a notch.

58. Observe the French Food Rules

French food rituals offer a daily exercise in teaching children how to delay gratification. Kids eat most meals in courses, rather than all at once. They taste foods, even ones they don't like—a form of coping with frustration. They wait to eat at mealtimes. If they get some chocolate in the morning, they typically don't eat it until the afternoon *goûter*. With practice, all of this gets much easier; in fact, it becomes natural and not arduous at all.

59. Let Them Eat Cake

Baking is a regular weekend activity for many French families, starting practically from the time kids can sit alone in a chair. The measuring and sequencing are excellent lessons in patience. And once the cake is made, families usually wait until the *goûter* to eat it. Everybody—parents included—aims to eat reasonable portions (they're trying to model restraint for their kids).

60. View Coping with Frustration as a Crucial Life Skill

....

French parents don't worry that they'll damage a child by frustrating her. *Au contraire*, they think a child can't be happy if she needs to have things instantly, and if she's constantly subject to her own whims. They believe that kids get pride and pleasure from being able to choose how they respond to things.

Teaching kids to handle frustration also makes them more resilient later on. Young children who are good at delaying gratification are more likely to grow into teenagers who can handle setbacks, and who are good at concentrating and reasoning. Consider it a French paradox: Trying to make kids happy all the time will make them less happy later on.

61. Cope Calmly with Tantrums

French parents are just as flummoxed and distressed by tantrums as the rest of us. They don't have a magic recipe to make the crying stop. What they generally agree on is: you shouldn't concede to an unreasonable demand. ("Above all, don't give in," one father tells me.) Tantrums don't change the rules

This doesn't mean that you should be cold. French parents say that kids are understandably angry when they can't have or do something. The parents try to show sympathy ("Who wouldn't want to have a cookie just before lunch?") and to let kids express their discontent. Some parents say they ask the child what she thinks a good solution is, given the constraints. If the child can calm down enough to talk, she'll often have some reasonable ideas—like having the same cookie as an afternoon snack.

Sometimes, giving an upset child more autonomy can change the mood and calm her down. Let her help you prepare dinner or serve herself. Be in touch with her rhythms. Don't expect an overtired child to go grocery shopping or out to dinner.

When the tantrum happens at home and goes on for too long, parents typically send the child to her room and tell her to come out when she's calm again. "If it's too loud I say, 'Go yell in your room.' But I understand that it makes her very angry," the mother of a five-year-old explains. Typically, "she goes into her room and yells, then she comes back out and does what I asked," this mom claims. If a child manages to come out calmly, parents respond positively and then everyone moves on.

In short, be calm and sympathetic without giving in.

62. Be Patient About Teaching Patience

Your child won't become an expert delayer in a day. Learning to wait is part of what the French call her *éducation*—an ongoing process of teaching her skills and values, which has nothing do with school. Be consistent. Whenever you start to waver, consider the alternative.

Chapter Seven

·····································

Free to Be
You and Moi

When a mother hovers over her child too much in France, someone is apt to say: "Just let him live his life!" French parents do a lot for their kids, but they don't try to clear away all obstacles, physical and emotional. Instead, they strive to treat children as independent beings who can, more and more as they get older, cope with challenges on their own.

This autonomy develops at a reasonable pace. Little French kids don't drive cars or operate heavy machinery. Parents supervise closely and judge when the child is ready to take the next step. But they believe that autonomy is crucial for children. When you treat kids as capable and trustworthy, they respond by taking on more responsibility and behaving better. And giving kids a bit of space can actually bring you closer.

63. Give Kids Meaningful Chores

Don't underestimate what children can do, with some guidance. It's quite normal for French three- and four-year-olds to help load the dishwasher after dinner, for instance. (Moms I know report no more than a few broken plates.) A friend of mine's six-year-old says her favorite activity is taking out the garbage all by herself. She also proudly describes the time when her mom stood outside a small shop and let her go inside alone to buy some lemons.

When done on a regular basis, these small acts of autonomy are very meaningful. Kids who play an active role in the household become more self-reliant, and learn that adults are not just there to serve them. Weirdly, children also find these activities fun. Obviously, the thrill won't last forever. But the idea that their contribution to the family matters probably will.

64. Build a Cadre

The cadre (meaning "frame" or "framework") is the mental image that French parents have about how best to raise kids. They strive to be very strict about a few key things—that's the frame. But inside the frame, they aim to give kids as much freedom as they can handle.

Parents decide which things they will be strict about. Parisians I've met often choose respect for others, how much screen time kids are allowed, and anything dealing with food. French children categorically aren't allowed to hit their parents.

You can apply the *cadre*'s cocktail of strictness and freedom to lots of different situations. Some that I've heard from French parents are:

- At bedtime you have to stay in your room, but inside your room you can do whatever you want.
- You can watch only two hours of television this weekend, but you choose when to use these two hours and you choose the DVD or the show you want to watch.

- You have to taste a bit of everything at a meal, but you don't have to eat it all
- When we go out, I can veto your outfit if it's inappropriate, but at home you can wear what you want.
- Most of the time you can't eat sweets, but you can at the afternoon snack.
- I don't buy nonnecessities on demand, but you can buy them with your pocket money. (French kids usually start getting monthly pocket money at about age seven. The typical amount corresponds to the child's age; i.e., a seven-year-old gets seven euros—about nine dollars—per month.)

65. Everybody Needs a Curse Word

There's a special one for French preschoolers: *caca boudin* (pronounced "caca boo-danh"). This literally translates as "poop sausage," but it's an all-purpose word that can mean "you wish," "bollocks," or "whatever." No one teaches his child to say *caca boudin*. Kids just pick it up from one another. Their parents might cringe a bit when they hear the phrase, but they tend not to ban it. Instead, they teach kids to wield it appropriately. Some tell their children they can say *caca boudin* only in the bathroom, or when they're alone with their friends. They can't say it to teachers, or at dinner. Kids are subject to lots of rules. Sometimes they just need to say *caca boudin*.

66. Hand Your Kids Over

If you can get a grandparent or trusted relative on board, let your child spend some time away from you. (French five-year-olds go on multiday class trips without any parents along, just teachers. During school holidays, they'll often spend a week or two alone with their grandparents.) Give your surrogate a few basic instructions, and try to project cheerful confidence when you're saying good-bye. Don't worry that she'll do things differently from you; your child mostly just needs tenderness, attention, and a bit of food. Start out with an overnight stay, then move up to a long weekend. "If everything goes well, he'll come back smarter," a French child psychiatrist explains[*] about kids aged three to five. "You'll find him changed, he will have learned to behave like a big boy. He'll gain in independence." I won't even start on the benefits to his parents.

67. Don't Become a Referee

The French ideal is for adults to avoid becoming the arbiters of all disputes—whether between siblings, playmates,

[*]In an article in a French parenting magazine titled "He's Going Away Without You, It's Good for Him!"

or new acquaintances in the sandbox. A father tells me that when his five-year-old twins argue, he asks them to suggest a solution. (They usually think of something, he says.) Teachers say they back off at recess, to give kids some much-needed freedom ("If we intervene all the time, they go a little nuts," one day-care minder explained).

French experts say that sibling rivalry is inevitable and that the arrival of a new baby is a genuine shock for an older child. In the latter case, "you must console him, help him express himself, reassure him, tell him that you understand his anxiety, his sorrow, his jealousy, show him that it's normal for him to have these feelings," one parenting book says.

68. Keep the Risks in Perspective

French parents know about choking hazards, allergies, and pedophiles. They take reasonable precautions. But they try not to obsess over far-flung scenarios. Instead of internalizing all worry, they believe that parents should speak to children about risks and teach them how to protect themselves. A French expert suggests explaining to a child as young as one that cars exist and that they're dangerous; thus he cannot cross a street without an adult.

There's a crucial difference between shielding a child from danger and cutting him off from the world. Remember that children gain confidence from overcoming difficulties and relying on their own resources. As one French writer warns, "To grow up without risk is to risk not growing up."

69. Don't Raise a Praise Addict

A French mother tells me that instead of saying "Bravo" when her five-year-old does something well, she prefers to ask, "Are you proud of yourself?" Like many French parents, she believes that children don't build self-esteem from being relentlessly assured that they're doing a good job. They build it from doing new things by themselves, and doing them well. Indeed, praising a child too much can be damaging. He'll become so eager to maintain your high opinion of him that he won't want to risk trying something new. Or he'll do things merely to get the brief high that comes from hearing "Bravo," but will lose motivation when you're not there to say it. Of course you should be encouraging (you don't want to underpraise either). Just don't overdo it.

70. Encourage Kids to Speak Well

Once a child can speak fluently, French parents and teachers don't automatically coo at everything he says. When he's wildly off topic, they say so, and steer him back. At the dinner table, they pay more attention when he says clever things and expresses himself well. This is meant to be constructive. They aim to turn the child into a good conversationalist, not a bore who blathers on. (He might get away with that at his grandmother's; it will be less charming later on dates.)

71. Expect the "Déclic"

The *déclic* (deh-kleek) is an aha moment when a child figures out how to do something important on his own. Something clicks. For young children, it can be the period when they become potty trained or work out how to make friends. For teenagers, it's the moment or period when they stop working to satisfy their parents and start working because they want to succeed for themselves. It's a welcome sign of maturity and autonomy. French parents often wait and hope for their children to have the *déclic*. Non-French parents do too. It's helpful to have a name for it.

72. Let Children Have a "Jardin Secret"

The French believe that everyone is entitled to a "secret garden"—a private realm. It's part of being an independent person. Even very involved parents accept that their children need privacy—particularly as they grow older—

and will have some secrets. They don't expect to know every detail of their children's lives. They do expect to know that, generally, everything is okay.

73. Respect a Child's Space, and He'll Respect Yours Too

Autonomy is something fundamental that your child needs. (Françoise Dolto said that by age six, a child should be able to do everything at home that concerns him.) Granting him autonomy—as he's ready—shows that you trust and respect him. It's an appeal to his higher self. Give him this, and he's more likely to respect what you need too. Ideally, as the French say, everyone in the family should get to live his life.

Chapter Eight

Cherchez la Femme

French mothers strive for a very particular kind of balance in their lives. It's not a keeping-plates-in-the-air balance. It's more like a balanced meal (you wouldn't want to eat just potatoes). The French ideal is that no one part of your life—not being a wife, a worker, or a mom—should eclipse the other parts. Even the most devoted *maman* is also supposed to devote energy and passion to things other than her children.

France has all kinds of social services that make it easier to do this. But mothers are also helped by a different approach to womanhood, guilt, and free time. The reigning view in France is that if the child is a woman's only goal, everyone suffers, including the child. Not all French moms manage to maintain just the right *équilibre*. But crucially, they keep it in mind.

74. Guilt Is a Trap

....

For American mothers, guilt can be like a tax you pay for being away from your child. It buys you some free time. As long as you feel guilty about leaving her, you can escape for a few hours. (Sociologists call this leisure time spent worrying "contaminated time.")

French moms understand the temptation to feel guilty. But they don't want to spoil their precious free time. Instead of embracing guilt, they try to push it away. When they meet up for drinks, they remind one another that "the perfect mother doesn't exist" and take pride in being able to detach from their children and relax. "When I'm there I give them one hundred percent, but when I'm off, I'm off," a mother of three explains.

75. Show Kids That You Have a Life Apart from Them

It's not enough for French mothers to have pleasures and interests apart from their children. They also want their kids to know about these things. They believe it's burdensome for a child to feel that she's the sole source of her mother's happiness and satisfaction. (A single mother I know in Paris told me she was going back to work partly for her daughter's sake.)

Frenchwomen want other adults to see that they have nonmom lives too. Even if they've spent the day folding tiny socks, they strive to resist talking at length about their children's toilet habits. They know that if you act (and dress) as if you have a fascinating inner life, you may soon find that you actually do—and that you feel more balanced as a result.

There are pragmatic reasons for having a life of your own. Some Frenchwomen drop out of the work force when they have kids, but many don't. Even those in stable marriages calculate that not making their own money would leave them financially vulnerable in case of divorce.

And they think that, sans paycheck, they'll lose status and decision-making power at home, and become less interesting to people outside of it.

76. Don't Attend Children's Birthdays

They're for kids. In Paris, from about age three, birthday parties and playdates are usually drop-offs. Parents don't feel they must supervise another adult's supervision of their child, or stick around to reassure the child herself. They make sure she's in good hands, and then they leave. Usually they're invited back for coffee or cocktails at the end. It's a practical way of coping with the fact that all parents are extremely busy, and that—while we're delighted that our kids get along—we're not all actually friends.

77. Lose the Baby Weight

For Frenchwomen, there's no better proof that they haven't morphed from *"femme"* to *"maman"* than getting back their prebaby figures, or some reasonable facsimile thereof. Parisiennes often aim to do this by three months postpartum.

It helps that they don't gain too much weight while they're pregnant, and that they're not permanently exhausted from night wake-ups. Many French moms also follow a nondeprivation diet as a matter of course. During the week they eat smallish portions, have the main meal at lunchtime, don't snack between meals, and avoid bread, pasta, and sugary foods. But on weekends (or on one weekend day) they eat freely. In other words, they don't vow never to eat lasagna or croissants again; they just save these for special occasions. Frenchwomen are in step with recent research showing that people have more self-control when they don't permanently exclude certain foods; they just tell themselves that they'll have them later. Studies also recommend closely monitoring your weight (Frenchwomen call this paying attention).

78. Don't Dress Like a Mom

Unless a Frenchwoman is actually holding a child, it's usually very hard to tell if she's a mother. There's no tell-tale look or type of pants. They don't sex it up to over-compensate (there's no French equivalent of MILF, because in France there's no reason why a mom wouldn't be sexy). But they don't walk around wearing sweatpants and scrunchies either. Instead, they seek an elegant middle ground. Frenchwomen don't feel selfish for caring about their appearance. (In the French edition of *Marie Claire*, a mother of three confesses that she's sometimes so busy *she wears unmatched bras and panties*.) Looking good improves morale and makes you feel more balanced. It just does.

79. Don't Become a "Taxi Mother"

Parisian mothers think it's perfectly reasonable to weigh the impact on their own quality of life when making choices for their child. A Frenchwoman who spends most of her free time shuttling her kids between extracurricular activities isn't seen as a devoted mom—she's viewed as someone who has dramatically lost her balance. Her sacrifice isn't even considered good for the kids. Yes, they may benefit from studying judo and taking piano lessons. But they also need to have unstructured time at home. A French psychologist says there's a crucial difference between being responsive and attentive to your child and becoming a "vending machine" who's always on.

80. You Can Be Happier Than Your Least Happy Child

Really you can. It doesn't mean that you're a bad person. It means that you're a separate person with your own needs and temperament. French mothers are deeply affected by their children's feelings. But they believe it's best to respond to an upset child with objectivity and calm. You're modeling the way you'd like her to feel.

Chapter Nine

Finding
Your Couple

French experts say that in the first few months after the baby is born, his parents should—indeed must— give themselves over to his care. They're in the *fusionelle* phase. Some call this, presidentially, the first hundred days.

But sometime around the three-month mark, parents are supposed to gradually make room for their own relationship again. There's no fixed schedule. No one expects them to abandon the baby and jump on a flight to Bali. It's more of a rebalancing in which they "relearn the contours of intimacy"—both physically and emotionally, and make space in the family home where they can be a couple.

81. Your Baby Doesn't Replace Your Husband

He's cuddly, he's adorable, and your mother loves him. But your child shouldn't permanently nudge your partner out of the picture. "The family is based on the couple. If it exists only through children, it withers," a French psychologist explains. In some families, the three-month mark is when the baby starts sleeping in his own room. (Until then he may have been in a bassinet in his parents' room, or even in their bed.) Long-term cosleeping is very rare in France, in part because it keeps things between Mom and Dad from getting back to normal.

The French famously believe that all healthy people— old people, ugly people, even new parents—have sex drives. A leading French parenting magazine says that if your libido hasn't returned by four to six months postpartum, you should seek professional help.

82. Your Bedroom Is Your Castle

Guard it carefully. Your child doesn't have the right to barge in whenever he wants. For starters, you need sleep. Explain to him that in the morning he must play in his room until it's very bright outside (or teach him to read a digital clock, and explain that he can't come in until the first number is an eight—or a seven on school days).

It's also important for him to understand—through tender gestures and closed doors—that there's a part of his parents' lives that doesn't involve him. "My parents' room was a sacred place, different from the rest of the house," one Frenchwoman recalls. "You didn't just walk in, you had to have a good reason. Between them there was an obvious pleasure that implied something unknown for us, the children." If your child believes he already has it all— that there's no mysterious adult world to aspire to—why should he bother growing up?

83. Be Clear-Eyed About How Hard Kids Are on a Relationship

The French swoon for babies, but they also talk about *"le baby-clash"*—the risk of couples' separating in the first two years, from the shock of becoming coparents and of losing their freedom. Experts don't have a magic solution, but say it's helpful to see this coming ("It's not us honey, it's le baby-clash!") and to discuss problems with each other. Reigniting intimacy helps too, as does clearly divvying up baby duties.

84. Pretend to Agree

No matter how misguided your partner's proclamations about the household rules are, don't contradict him in front of the kids. Wait and speak in private. He should do the same for you. You'll build complicity with your spouse. And since the rules aren't up for discussion, they'll have more force. You'll both seem more authoritative to the children, and they'll be reassured by the impression that there's something solid at the family's core.

85. 50/50 Isn't the Gold Standard

Feeling entitled to absolute equality in housework and child care can be a recipe for resentment and rage. Fifty-fifty rarely happens. Try tempering your feminist theory with some old-fashioned French pragmatism. Frenchwomen would love their partners to do more, but many make peace with a division of labor that isn't equal but that more or less works. They try to weigh equality against having a husband who's calm and destressed after his Saturday morning soccer match. And they've discovered that there's less conflict when everyone has his or her own tasks to perform at home—even if the actual hours involved aren't equal. Paradoxically, if you're less angry, you might want to have more sex, and he might do more around the house as a result.

86. Treat Men Like a Separate Species

Take the edge off inequality even more by treating men the way that many Frenchwomen do—as adorably hapless creatures who, in most cases, are biologically incapable of keeping track of the kids' inoculation schedules. Of course they come home with the wrong cereal and with strawberries that look as if they've been beaten with a mallet. They're men! They just can't help it. (One Frenchwoman told me, with mock exasperation, that her husband makes only his side of the bed.) Frenchwomen advise trying not to throw a tantrum when you come home from a business trip to find your home besieged by dirty laundry. It's possible that the poor fellow was actually doing his best.

87. Men, Praise Mom for Her Mastery of the Mundane

Centuries of expert courtship have taught Frenchmen that you cannot overpraise a woman. They try to compensate for their shortcomings at home by marveling at the dull and time-consuming tasks their partners perform and by confessing that such multitasking is beyond them. (When said gallantly, this sounds less patronizing than you'd expect.) If the woman doesn't have a paying job, Frenchmen are wise enough never to ask: What did you *do* all day?

88. Maintain Some Mystery About Yourself

Don't have an extramarital affair, or do terrible things in secret (it may surprise you to know that ordinary French citizens rarely cheat; it's French presidents who tend not to be terribly faithful). But keep a bit of mystery in your marriage, *à la française.* Let there be innuendo, knowing glances, and things left unsaid. It's okay to flirt with others too. Realize that—unlike in Hollywood scripts—you can feel energized by these interactions without their leading inexorably to adultery and death.

89. Make Evenings Adult Time

After the stories, songs, and cuddles, French parents are firm about bedtime. They believe that having some kid-free time in the evenings is not an occasional privilege; it's a fundamental human right. Ditto with spending the occasional evening out or escaping for a restorative long weekend *à deux*. The French don't have an equivalent of "date night." When they can, they just go out—the way our parents used to. They consider a solid and loving marriage to be essential to the happy functioning of the whole family. Explain this honestly to the kids; they'll get it.

90. Don't Put a Teepee in Your Living Room

The French know that it's hard to enjoy adult time when you're staring at a miniature kitchen. They typically don't let children's toys and games reside permanently in the living room. Make a family ritual of putting them back in the kids' rooms before bedtime. Have a (non-Technicolor) box in the living room where you can hide stray Legos and doll extremities. Don't let baby-proofing be your dominant interior design motif.

Chapter Ten

Just Say
"Non"

A battle cry of French parenting is: It's me who decides (*C'est moi qui décide*). Parents say—and occasionally shout—this phrase to remind everyone who's in charge or to shift the balance of power back in their favor. Just uttering it is fortifying. (Try saying it, even in French. You'll feel your back stiffen.)

To be the decider, you don't have to be an ogre. French parents don't want to turn their kids into obedient robots. But they still agree with Jean-Jacques Rousseau's contention, made 250 years ago, that perpetual negotiations are bad for kids. "The worst education is to leave him floating between his will and yours, and to dispute endlessly between you and him as to which of the two will be the master."

91. Say "No" with Conviction

The French didn't invent *non*. But they're especially good at saying it. They don't worry that blocking a child will limit his creativity or crush his spirit. They believe that kids blossom best inside limits, and that it's reassuring to know that a grown-up is steering the ship.

The French *non* is convincing partly because parents don't say it constantly. They believe that a few strategically administered *no*s have a better chance of registering with kids than a blizzard of them. They're consistently strict about a few key things.

But the real secret is the unambivalent delivery. Kids can tell when you really mean no and you won't back down. You don't have to shout it. Just look directly at the child, kneeling down if you have to, and explain the rule with calm confidence. This takes some practice. When you get your *no* right, you'll feel it. You won't just sound more authoritative to your child; you will actually believe yourself to be the boss.

92. Say "Yes" as Often as You Can

The French believe that another key to having authority with your child is to say yes as often as you can. (One expert points out that *authority* has the same root as *authorize*.) It takes some recalibrating to make your default answer become yes. But doing this has a calming effect. The child feels more respected, and she gets to satisfy her need to do things for herself. Of course, total freedom would be overwhelming. The ideal French scenario is that the child asks permission to do something, and the parent grants it.

93. *Explain the Reason Behind the Rule*

When you say no, you should always explain why not. You're not trying to scare your child into obeying you. Rather, you want to create a world that's coherent and predictable to him, and to show that you respect his autonomy and intelligence.

If a situation is dangerous, act first and give your reason afterward. Always be matter of fact: you don't want your explanation to sound like a negotiation (it's not). Sometimes it helps to refresh kids on the rules. One French mom says that as soon as she walks into the supermarket, she reminds her two girls that they're there to buy necessities for the house, not toys or candy. She says she's been so consistent about applying this, the girls don't even ask for these extras anymore. (They can choose to buy them with their pocket money.)

When speaking to kids, French parents will often use the language of rights: "You don't have the right to bite Pierre." This implies that there's a coherent system of rules and that the child *does* have the right to do other things.

94. Sometimes Your Child Will Hate You

French psychologists say that kids' desires are practically endless. Your job as a parent is to stop this chain by sometimes saying no. The child will probably get angry when you do this. She might even temporarily hate you. This isn't a sign that you're a terrible parent. "If the parent isn't there to stop him, then he's the one who's going to have to stop himself or not stop himself, and that's much more anxiety-provoking," one psychologist explains. In other words, if you need your child to like you all the time, you simply cannot do your job. Be strong and your child will, as the French say, "find her place."

95. Dedramatize

This word comes up a lot in France when it comes to dealing with upset or cranky kids of all ages. The idea is that you should drain some intensity from conflictual moments by responding calmly to them, or lightening the mood with a joke.

Avoid castigating your child in front of others. One French mom told me she suspected that her teenage daughter was smoking cigarettes during a sleepover, but she waited until the friend left the next morning before mentioning it. "If you make a scene, your child will stop talking to you," she explained.

Aim to have authority without losing your connection with the child. If you're so angry that you need time to cool off, say so. "I don't think the world of children is so far from the world of adults. They're capable of understanding everything," this mom said.

96. You're Not Disciplining, You're Educating

The next time your child speaks with a mouth full of pasta, remember that you're gradually teaching her table manners, in the same way that you would teach her to do math.

In other words, the learning doesn't happen all at once. As the French say, you're not disciplining, you're giving the child an *éducation*, an ongoing process that starts when kids are very young. Unlike discipline, *éducation* (which has nothing to do with school) is something parents imagine themselves to be doing all the time. Reminding yourself that you're educating will help you feel less disrespected and angry when the occasional slice of cucumber lands on your lap.

Don't jump on your child for every offense. The French call a small act of naughtiness a *bêtise* (pronounced beh-teeze). Having this word helps keep the crime in perspective. When your child jumps on the couch or swipes a piece of bread off the counter before dinner, she's just done a *bêtise*. All kids do them sometimes. Save your punishments for the felonies. It will help her learn what's important.

97. Do the Big Eyes

In France, one suitable response to a *bêtise* is to give a child "the big eyes." It's a disapproving, owl-like look that serves as a warning. It means that you saw what she did, and she should watch her step. "The important thing is that she knows she's breaking a rule," one mother told me.

98. Give Kids Time to Comply

You're running a family, not a military battalion. Don't expect your child to jump as soon as you issue an order. Explain what you'd like her to do, then watch and wait for her to comply. Obviously you're applying pressure. But you also want to give her autonomy over how and at what speed she complies. It's more likely to be an effective long-term lesson if she feels that she has some say in the matter too.

99. Punish Rarely, but Make It Matter

To be *puni* in a French family is a big deal. It's not something that usually happens every night at dinner. Experts say a punishment should be administered immediately and matter-of-factly, without malice. Parents typically send a naughty child to her room to "marinate," or think on it, and tell her to come out when she's calm and ready to talk. For older kids, the punishment is often a few days without TV, computers, or video games, or taking away the child's phone for a week. Parents say they're careful to warn kids before punishing them, and to follow through on their threats. They also try to be fair on the other end—by returning the phone on the promised day. After a conflict, they say it's the parent's role to reestablish the connection, for instance by suggesting that they play a favorite game together. Teach the child that after the storm comes calm.

100. Sometimes There's Nothing You Can Do

Know when to fold 'em. There are times when nothing works, and you have to wait it out. Remember, you're on a long-term mission to educate. You don't have to win every battle.

Favorite Recipes from the Parisian Crèche

These dishes are eaten by children aged three and under who attend Paris's public day cares. They're typically cooked from scratch by in-house chefs at each center, then served as four-course meals composed of an appetizer, a main course and side dish, a cheese course, and then a fruit dessert (kids under twelve months have only two courses). A crèche nutritionist has adapted the quantities for family dining; each recipe serves two adults and two children.

Carottes Râpées à L'orange
Grated Carrots with Orange

This dish can be prepared just before serving
or allowed to marinate overnight.

3 carrots

2 tablespoons canola oil

Juice of 1 orange

⅛ clove crushed garlic

Pinch of salt

Grate the carrots.

Mix the oil, juice, garlic and salt in a small bowl.

Pour this mixture over the grated carrots and toss.

Veloute D'artichaut à La Crème

Creamy Artichoke Soup

1 large Idaho or russet potato

2 shallots, finely chopped

2 tablespoons olive oil

6 canned or bottled artichoke bottoms, diced

Water (about 2 cups)

Salt

2 tablespoons crème fraîche (or sour cream)

Herbs (parsley, basil, or cilantro), chopped

Wash and peel the potato. Dice it into large pieces.

In a large pan or casserole dish, sauté the shallots in a little olive oil.

Add the potatoes and the artichokes. Sauté them for 2 to 3 minutes.

Cover the vegetables with water, add some salt, and cook for about 40 minutes (or 20 minutes in a pressure cooker).

After cooking, add the cream and mix well. If you prefer a smooth consistency, use a hand mixer to blend the soup.

Keep the soup warm until you're ready to eat it. Add a pinch of chopped herbs before serving.

Brocoli Braisé

Braised Broccoli

1 pound broccoli, fresh or frozen
Salt
1 tablespoon unsalted butter

Steam fresh broccoli for 4 to 5 minutes or submerge it in boiling water for 5 to 6 minutes. Steam frozen broccoli for 8 to 10 minutes or submerge it in boiling water for 10 to 12 minutes. The broccoli should be firm, not mushy. Save some of the cooking water. Drain the broccoli well and add a few pinches of salt.

Melt the butter in a pan. Sauté the broccoli in the butter over medium heat for 5 minutes, until it's tender. If the broccoli is still too firm, moisten it with a bit of the cooking water.

Potage Complet Lentilles

Complete-Meal Lentil Soup

2 shallots, chopped

Olive oil

2 cups lentils

*2 medium potatoes, peeled, washed, and chopped into
    medium-sized pieces*

5 cups cold water

1 clove garlic, chopped

Black pepper

½ teaspoon cumin

2 medium carrots, peeled

Salt

¼ cup crème fraîche (or sour cream)

2 ounces boneless chicken breasts, finely diced

Parsley, chopped

In a large saucepan, sauté the shallots in some olive oil, add the lentils and potatoes, and cover with the cold water. Add the garlic, black pepper, cumin, and carrots.

Bring to a boil and simmer, covered, over medium heat for 45 minutes or until the potatoes and lentils are soft. Add more water if needed. Season with salt. Stir the crème fraîche into the lentils (you can mix in less cream if you want, or just add a dollop to each bowl before serving). While the lentils are cooking, use a sauté pan to brown the chicken in a little olive oil. Pour the soup into bowls, then add some chicken and a pinch of parsley to each.

Saumon à La Créole

Salmon Creole

This dish has become a staple in Parisian crèches thanks to the many in-house chefs who hail from the French Caribbean.

1 medium onion, chopped

1½ tablespoons sunflower or olive oil

14½ ounces diced tomatoes, canned or fresh

½ teaspoon thyme, chopped

1 bay leaf

Parsley, chopped

Salt and pepper

3 to 4 medium-sized salmon fillets, fresh or frozen

Juice of 1 lemon

Preheat the oven to 425°F.

In a large pan, sauté the onion in the oil.

Add the tomatoes, thyme, bay leaf, parsley, and salt and pepper. Cover and let simmer for 15 minutes.

Place the salmon fillets in an ovenproof pan. (If you're using frozen fillets, first defrost them in a microwave oven.)

Squeeze the lemon juice over the salmon, then spoon the tomato mixture on top of that. Bake in the oven for 20 to 30 minutes, or until thoroughly cooked. Before serving, remove all the bones and the bay leaf, and add a pinch of fresh parsley or chives to each plate. Serve the salmon with rice and a side of vegetables (braised broccoli is recommended).

Flan de Courgettes

Zucchini Flan

3 medium-sized zucchini

2 shallots, finely chopped

2 tablespoons olive oil

4 eggs

A bit less than 1 cup crème fraîche (or sour cream)

¼ teaspoon salt

¼ teaspoon ground nutmeg

¾ cup grated cheese (Gruyère or Swiss)

Preheat the oven to 350°F.

Wash and peel the zucchini. Cook them whole, either by steaming them for 9 minutes or by submerging them in boiling water for 15 minutes.

Drain the zucchini well. Cut them into thin round slices.

Sauté the shallots in the olive oil.

In a bowl, mix the eggs, crème fraîche, shallots, salt, and nutmeg. Don't overmix.

Line a square or rectangular pan with parchment paper (if you have it).

Arrange a layer of zucchini in the bottom of the pan.

Spoon the egg mixture over the zucchini until it's completely covered. Add another layer of zucchini and cover with the egg mixture again. Keep doing this until you've used up all the ingredients.

Sprinkle the cheese over the top and bake for 30 to 40 minutes.

Optional (but highly recommended): Top each serving of zucchini flan with a bit of warm tomato coulis (see recipe below).

Tomato Coulis

4 large ripe tomatoes (or about 11 ounces canned diced
   tomatoes)
3 tablespoons olive oil
1 clove garlic, peeled and left whole
½ teaspoon thyme, chopped

½ teaspoon parsley, chopped

1 bay leaf

½ tablespoon sugar

Salt and pepper

For fresh tomatoes: Cut the skin at the base of the tomatoes and plunge them into boiling water for 30 seconds so you can easily remove the skin. Peel, seed, and dice them.

Heat the oil in a saucepan. Add the garlic, thyme, parsley, bay leaf, tomatoes, sugar, and salt and pepper. Cover and simmer on low heat for 20 to 30 minutes.

Remove the garlic clove and bay leaf before serving.

Purée de Poire et Banane

Pear and Banana Puree

2 large or 3 small soft pears
2 bananas
Juice of ½ lemon
¼ cup water

Wash and peel the pears and bananas. Cut them into pieces.

In a medium-sized saucepan, cook them with the lemon juice and water for 15 to 20 minutes over low heat. Mix occasionally with a spoon.

Take the mixture off the heat and allow it to cool for a few minutes.

When it's no longer steaming, pour it into small cups. Cover and refrigerate them until mealtime.

Pomme au Four à la Cannelle

Baked Apple with Cinnamon

*4 apples (any cooking apples, including Granny Smith
or Golden Delicious)*
1⅓ tablespoons unsalted butter
4 teaspoons sugar
Cinnamon

Preheat the oven to 350°F.

Wash and core the apples (leave a bit of core at the
bottom if you can).

Put a knob of butter and a teaspoon of sugar in the
center of each apple. Sprinkle same cinnamon over
the top.

Put about ⅛ inch of water in a baking dish (to keep
the apples from sticking), place the apples on top.

Cook for 20 to 30 minutes, until the center of the
apples melt.

Remove the apples from the water. Serve them
warm or cold.

Gâteau Chocolat

Chocolate Cake

Butter and flour to grease the pan

5 ounces dark baking chocolate

7 tablespoons unsalted butter (a bit less than 1 stick)

6 tablespoons powdered sugar

6 tablespoons flour

3 large or 4 small eggs, separated

Salt

Optional: whipped cream or crème fraîche

Preheat the oven to 350°F. Grease and flour a 9-inch round cake pan.

In a saucepan over very low heat, slowly melt the chocolate and butter.

Remove the chocolate mixture from the heat. While mixing with a wooden spoon, sprinkle in the powdered sugar, then the flour. Add the egg yolks one by one and stir.

In a separate bowl, beat the egg whites with a pinch of salt until they form stiff peaks.

Slowly fold the egg whites into the chocolate mixture. Do not overmix.

Immediately pour the batter into the pan. Bake for 30 minutes.

Let the cake cool. Serve with a dollop of whipped cream.

Sample
Weekly Lunch Menu
from the
Parisian Crèche

	Appetizer	*Main Course*
MONDAY		
UNDER 12 MONTHS		mashed boneless filet of hake with lemon sauce
12 TO 18 MONTHS	tomato salad with lemon and herbs	chopped boneless filet of hake with lemon sauce
18 MONTHS TO 3 YEARS	tomato salad with lemon and herbs	boneless filet of hake with lemon-butter sauce
TUESDAY		
UNDER 12 MONTHS		mashed turkey with basil sauce
12 TO 18 MONTHS	cream of leek soup	chopped turkey with basil sauce
18 MONTHS TO 3 YEARS	cream of leek soup	chopped turkey with basil sauce
WEDNESDAY		
UNDER 12 MONTHS		mashed slow-cooked lamb with carrot and tomatoes
12 TO 18 MONTHS	grated red cabbage with soft white cheese (fromage blanc)	chopped slow-cooked lamb with carrots and tomatoes
18 MONTHS TO 3 YEARS	grated red cabbage with soft white cheese (fromage blanc)	slow-cooked lamb with carrots and tomatoes
THURSDAY		
UNDER 12 MONTHS		finely chopped ham
12 TO 18 MONTHS	Macedonian salad (green beans, carrots, celery, and flageolet beans in a lemon sauce)	chopped ham
18 MONTHS TO 3 YEARS	wheat, tomato, and green pepper salad	gratin of endives and ham
FRIDAY		
UNDER 12 MONTHS		mashed filet of boneless salmon in lemon-dill sauce
12 TO 18 MONTHS	finely grated organic carrot salad	chopped filet of boneless salmon in lemon-dill sauce
18 MONTHS TO 3 YEARS	grated organic carrot salad	filet of boneless salmon in lemon-dill sauce

Side Dish	Cheese	Dessert
organic spinach puree		sugarless apple-strawberry puree
organic spinach puree	Coulommiers cheese (a soft cow's milk cheese that resembles Brie)	sugarless apple-strawberry puree
organic spinach with Béchamel sauce	Mimolette cheese (a hard orange cow's milk cheese)	sugarless apple-strawberry puree
puree of zucchini		sugarless pear and organic apple puree
puree of zucchini	Chanteneige cheese (a spreadable white cheese)	fresh kiwi
ratatouille with rice	Chanteneige cheese	fresh kiwi
puree of mushrooms		banana-rhubarb compote with sugar
puree of mushrooms	white Tomme cheese (a firm cow's milk cheese)	banana-rhubarb compote with sugar
couscous	white Tomme cheese	banana-rhubarb compote with sugar
puree of fresh endives		puree of cooked clementine and organic apples
puree of fresh endives	Roquefort cheese	fresh clementine
	Roquefort cheese	fresh clementine
puree of broccoli		puree of cooked organic apples
puree of broccoli	chèvre (goat's milk cheese)	baked organic apples
twist pasta with butter	chèvre (goat's milk cheese)	baked organic apples

Acknowledgments

This book exists thanks to Ann Godoff, Suzanne Gluck, Marianne Velmans, and Virginia Smith—who valiantly edited the manuscript while trapped by a hurricane.

Thanks to nutritionist Sandra Merle at the Direction des Familles et de la Petite Enfance in Paris for providing the recipes, and for tolerating my many questions about them. I'm also grateful to Claire Smith, who worked tirelessly to test them (and to baby Kate and others, who were made to eat them). My thanks to Adam Kuper and Sapna Gupta for their comments on the manuscript, and to Sarah Hutson, Aislinn Casey, and Kate Samano. To my indefatigable illustrator, Margaux Motin: thank you for making my legs look twice as long as they actually are.

I'm extremely thankful to readers of *Bringing Up Bébé* who wrote to me with questions, comments, stories, and encouragement. Your enthusiasm inspired this book. *Merci* to the many French parents who allowed me to ask them questions and observe them in their natural habitats, including Frédérique Souverain, Ingrid Callies, Christophe Delin, Solange Martin, Esther Zajdenweber, Cécile Agon, Christophe Dunoyer, Aurèle Cariès, Benjamin Barda, and Véronique Bouruet-Aubertot.

The paradox of writing a parenting book is that you must avoid your own family in order to finish it. My gratitude, always, to Bonnie and Hank. Thank you to Leo, Leila, and Joey for their patience (and love). Most of all, thank you to Simon—their father and my husband. *Après toi, le déluge.*

Bibliography

Badinter, Elisabeth. *The Conflict: How Modern Motherhood Undermines the Status of Women*. New York: Metropolitan Books, 2012.

Baumeister, Roy F., and John Tierney. *Willpower: Rediscovering the Greatest Human Strength*. New York: Penguin Press, 2011.

Bloom, Paul. "Moral Life of Babies." *New York Times Magazine*, May 3, 2010. http://www.nytimes.com/2010/05/09/magazine/09babies-t.html?pagewanted=all.

Bronson, Po, and Ashley Merryman. *NurtureShock: New Thinking About Children*. New York: Twelve, 2009.

Brunet, Christine, and Nadia Benlakhel. *C'est pas bientôt fini ce caprice? Les calmer sans s'énerver*. Paris: Albin Michel, 2005.

Carroll, Raymonde. *Cultural Misunderstandings: The French-American Experience*. Chicago: University of Chicago Press, 1990.

Delahaye, Marie-Claude. *Livre de bord de la future maman*. Paris: Marabout, 2007.

De Leersnyder, Hélène. *L'enfant et son sommeil*. Paris: Robert Laffont, 1998.

Dolto, Françoise. *Lorsque l'enfant Paraît, Tome 1*. Paris: Éditions du Seuil, 1977.

Dolto, Françoise, and Danielle Marie Lévy. *Parler juste aux enfants*. Paris: Gallimard, 2002.

Famili.fr. "La reprise de la sexualité après bébé." http://www.fa mili.fr/,la-reprise-de-la-sexualite-apres-bebe,438,10193.asp.

Famili.fr. "Devenir parents et rester amants?" http://www.famili .fr/,devenir-parents-et-rester-amants,599,280849.asp.

Gallais, Marie. "Impossible de s'occuper seule." *Parents,* October 2012, 99–100.

Gravillon, Isabelle, et al. "Nos enfants sont-ils trop protégés?" *Enfant Magazine,* September 2012, 56–57.

Haberfeld, Ingrid. "Quel est l'impact du stress sur la grossesse?" *Parents,* April 2012, 60–61.

Heckman, James J. "Schools, Skills and Synapses." http://www .heckmanequation.org/content/resource/presenting-heckman-equation.

Henry, Dominique. "Il part sans vous, et c'est bon pour lui!" *Famili,* August/September 2012, 104–6.

Kahneman, Daniel, and Alan B. Krueger. "Developments in the Measurement of Subjective Well-Being." *Journal of Economic Perspectives* 20, 1 (2006): 3–24.

Marcelli, Daniel. *Il est permis d'obéir*. Paris: Albin Michel, 2009.

Marchi, Catherine. "12 conseils pour faire le Bonheur de votre enfant." *Parents,* August 2010, 52–54.

Merle, Sandra, interview with the author, September 20, 2012.

Mindell, Jodi, et al. "Behavioral Treatment of Bedtime Problems and Night Wakings in Young Children: AASM Standards of Practice." *Sleep* 29 (2006): 1263–76.

Mischel, Walter, interview with the author, July 20, 2010.

Mon Enfant à l'école maternelle. http://cache.media.education.gouv
.fr/file/Espace_parent/35/9/Guide_pratique_des_parents
_ecole_maternelle_227359.pdf.

National Institutes of Health. "Child Care Linked to Assertive,
Noncompliant, and Aggressive Behaviors: Vast Majority of
Children Within Normal Range." July 16, 2003.

Ochs, Elinor, and Carolina Izquierdo. "Responsibility in Childhood: Three Developmental Trajectories." *Ethos* 37, no. 4
(2009): 391–413.

Ollivier, Debra. *What French Women Know About Love, Sex, and
Other Matters of Heart and Mind.* New York: G. P. Putnam's
Sons, 2009.

Pernoud, Laurence. *J'élève mon enfant.* Paris: Editions Horay,
2007.

Pinella, Teresa, and Leann L. Birch. "Help Me Make It Through
the Night: Behavioral Entrainment of Breast Fed Infants
Sleep Patterns." *Pediatrics* 91, no. 2 (1993): 436–43.

Pleux, Didier. "Enfants tyrans: un peu de bon sens!" Interview
by Doctissimo.fr. http://www.doctissimo.fr/html/psychologie/
mag_2003/mag1024/ps_7167_enfants_tyrans_bon_sens_itw
.htm.

Programme National Nutrition Santé. *La santé vient en mangeant
et en bougeant.* 2004.

Rossant, Lyonel, and Jacqueline Rossant-Lumbroso. *Votre Enfant: Guide à l'usage des parents.* Paris: Robert Laffont, 2006.

Rousseau, Jean-Jacques. *Emile, or On Education.* Translated by
Allan Bloom. New York: Basic Books, 1979.

Senior, Jennifer. "All Joy and No Fun." *New York*, July 12, 2010.

Sethi, Anita, Walter Mischel, J. Lawrence Aber, Yuichi Shoda, and Monica Larrea Rodriguez. "The Role of Strategic Attention Deployment in Development of Self-Regulation: Predicting Preschoolers' Delay of Gratification from Mother-Toddler Interactions." *Developmental Psychology* 36, no. 6 (November 2000): 767–77.

Thirion, Marie, and Marie-Josèphe Challamel. *Le sommeil, le rêve et l'enfant: De la naissance à l'adolescence.* Paris: Albin Michel, 2002.

Thompson, Caroline. Interview by author. April 20, 2010.

Twenge, Jean M., W. Keith Campbell, and Craig A. Foster. "Parenthood and Marital Satisfaction: A Meta-Analytic Review." *Journal of Marriage and Family* 65, 3 (August 2003): 574–83.

Vaineau, Anne-Laure. *5 conseils pour éviter le baby-clash.* http://www.psychologies.com/Famille/Etre-parent/Equilibre-du-couple/Articles-et-Dossiers/5-conseils-pour-eviter-le-baby-clash.

Warner, Judith. "How to Raise a Child." *New York Times,* July 27, 2012. http://www.nytimes.com/2012/07/29/books/review/teach-your-children-well-by-madeline-levine.html?pagewanted=all.

Winter, Pam. *Engaging Families in the Early Childhood Development Story; Neuroscience and Early Childhood Development: Summary of Selected Literature and Key Messages for Parenting.* Education Services Australia Ltd. As the legal entity for the Ministerial Council for Education, Early Childhood Development and Youth Affairs, 2010.